POWER OF WORDS
Voices of Poetry

2011 WINNERS
of Poetry Matters Literary Prize

Introduction by Valerie Wooten
Compiled by Lucinda Clark

The Power Of Words: Voices of Poetry

ISBN-13: 9780984014200 print
ISBN-13: 9780982140789 e-book
Library of Congress Control Number: 2011916075

P.R.A. Publishing
P.O. Box 211701
Martinez, Georgia 30917
www.prapublishing.com

Cover design by CreateSpace
Printed in the United States of America

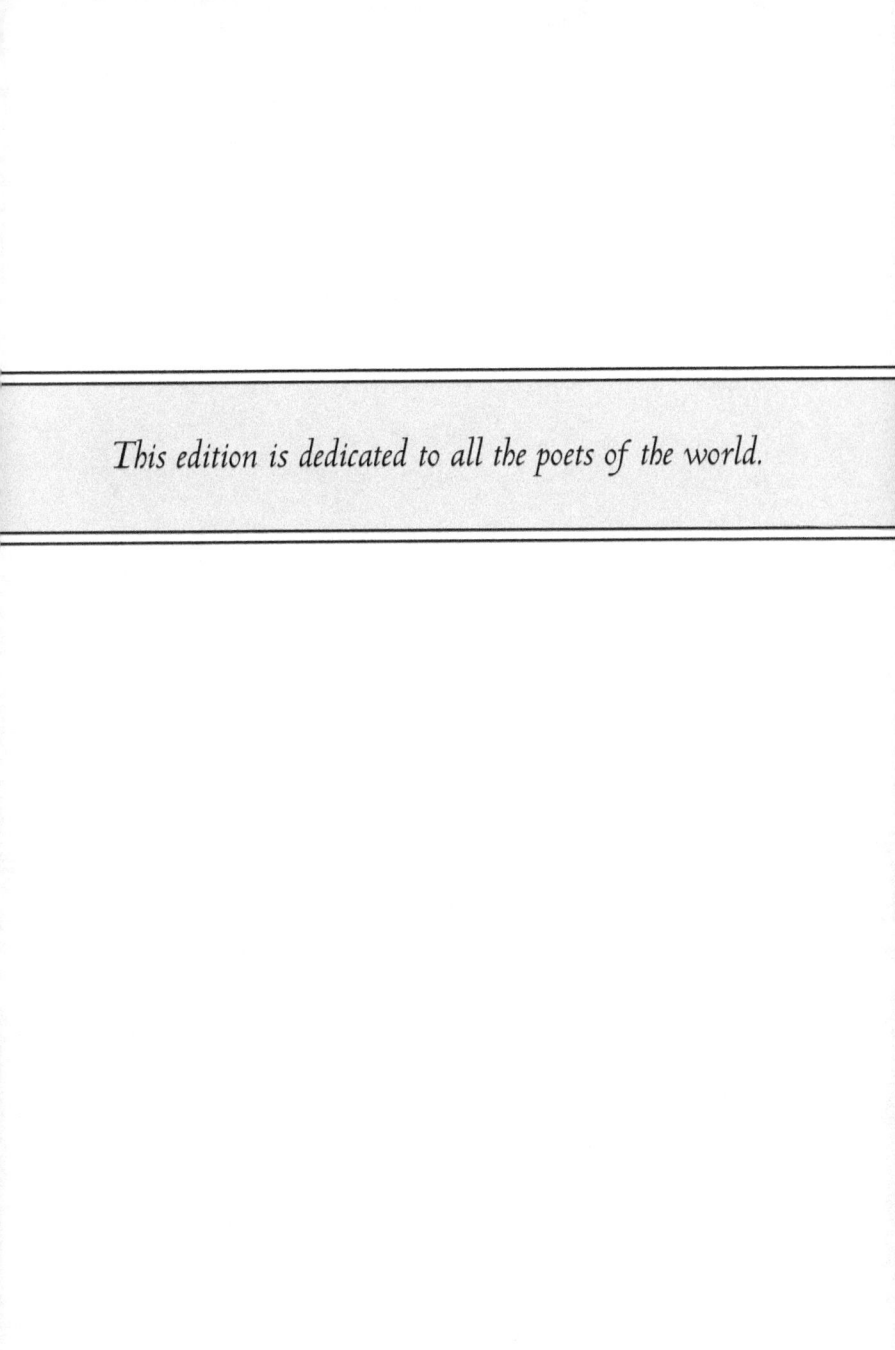

This edition is dedicated to all the poets of the world.

Acknowledgements

Poetry, this literary art form stands the test of time, why? Because poets cannot help themselves. They must put to paper what they experience and poetry lovers encourage them to share what they write.

We, the producers of this prize want to thank the poetry lovers who support us. Especially the judges, sponsors notably; Friends of Columbia County Library and Center for Primary Care.

Finally, thanks to Dr. Anthony Kellman at Augusta State University for believing in the intern he referred to us. She was instrumental in putting this edition together. Valerie wrote the introduction and assisted with layout and design. We hope she follows her dreams and one day is able to see her name in lights.

TABLE OF CONTENTS

Introduction

The writing of this introduction was no easy task. You would think it would be. "Talk about the experience you had in putting this anthology together," my publisher tells me enthusiastically. I was excited at first. I re-read the poems and began writing this tale of traveling through mountains and forests of words and experiences; I dressed up metaphors and practiced clever uses of alliteration...blah, blah, blah. It just didn't fit. I switched gears and started writing about the process it took in putting together a book from beginning to end, but I added too many details and the task seemed so daunting written down that I knew I would lose the reader.

Truth is I've gone through many things personally in conjunction with putting this book together, which contributed to the loss of the perfect intro. September, I was a bridesmaid and part time wedding planner for my best friend's wedding. That same night, she revealed to me that she had cancer. The first week of October, my Uncle called all the family together from out of town because his lung cancer was progressing rapidly. A week later my 4 year old had an asthma attack when he's never had any respiratory problems before. He had to spend the night in the hospital. My uncle passed October 18. I was a wreck. It wasn't until I had a quick moment of stillness and silence that the words flowed onto the computer screen.

I've had a love/hate relationship with poetry for as long as I can remember. The thing I love about poetry is how emotionally deep you can take a poem. You are allowed to dive deep within yourself and pull out emotions and thoughts that you had never uttered before without feeling ashamed or having to explain yourself. Poetry allows you to be free. Sometimes a period behind a sentence is too much and poetry says it's okay if you don't want to use it. Sometimes you don't feel linear-lining every sentence beneath the other one with all lines left aligned on the paper. Sometimes your feelings are jarring and erratic and words need to be right aligned or bigger than the word next to it. Poetry gives the poet this outlet to do as he/she pleases and it is ok.

Another love I have for poetry is how it transcends age and time. People from all walks of life can relate. It is a universal language. Just as in this anthology, there are poems from middle school age students to senior adults. It is hard to tell the difference. That is poetry-the ability to speak to the heart and not the head.

My hate for poetry is how abstract it can be. Instead of simply stating the message, poets often tuck and roll it into this flowery language and metaphors that force me to think and find a connection with. Just tell me what you want me to know; I don't want to ponder the meaning.

This anthology is one to be devoured though. You have your abstract poems that force you to go deeper than the surface layer and then there are poems that directly tell you the meaning. That's what I love most about this book. It's not about the hours deciding which font to use or trying to figure out a front cover that's appealing to the eye, but it is the words inside of the book. Yes those things are important, but it is the voice of each poet that speaks to the reader's heart, as you read this, it is the stories of those young and old that collectively come together to bask in the sunlight of your mind, and it is the possibility to change lives, one poem at a time. This is the beauty of poetry.

Valerie Wooten-Augusta State University

FIRST PLACE WINNERS

LIFE IS A ROAD

Life is like a road
Twisting and turning
Not knowing where it's leading you
The powerful God Dagda determining our paths-
Every decision I make leads me onto a new road
Sometimes I get stuck not knowing where to turn
I wait until the light turns green
Telling me to go
Life is bumpy
We all make wrongs and rights
While getting lost along the way
My future depends on the decisions I make
I go up a hill at some points
Feeling like I've chosen right
Until I go down learning from my mistakes
Making the wrong turn
I know I'll get lost
Finding my way out will not be easy
But I know my future is bright
I have to get past the bumpy part
To get to the smooth part
I go through ups and downs everyday
But I know it will be good
Until I reach the end of the road
You have to go through the twists and turns
To get to the path that holds your future
All the trouble
Is worth it at the end

Danielle O'Brien
Plano, TX

THE TOY DANCER

Night was coming.
Day was leaving.
Stars were shining.
A time for dreaming.

In a small house
Of a little girl,
A toy dancer came alive
With the tiniest little twirl.

Pointed, black shoes
And a shiny, red dress
She had a tiara on her head
And was practicing her arabesque.

Then all of a sudden
To the dancer's surprise
There stood the little girl
Who couldn't believe her eyes.

For a magic toy,
When life is caught,
It becomes pale as the moon
And to the ground it drops.

The ballerina did just that
And as for the child,
She thought she was dreaming
And went back to bed with a smile.

Who would help the poor dancer
Laying down on the table?
None other than the toy man
Who came with the toy stable.

He watched the toy dancer
Every night she danced.
He wondered how to save her
So he could once again be entranced.

He came up with a plan
And it was a good one indeed.
He would kiss the ballerina
And hope he would succeed.

He sat on his fine brown horse
And made jumps from here to there.
He approached the toy dancer
With fair skin and beautiful hair.

The toy man stroked her cheek
And knelt down to kiss her
And as his wooden lips touched hers,
She became a glittery blur.

The toy dancer disappeared
And the toy man began to sob.
But the dancer appeared behind him
And tapped him to make him stop.

He looked up behind him
And his eyes grew wide.
The dancer hugged her rescuer
And the man felt pride.

The night grew to a close
And the sun came out.
A little girl woke up
And she began to shout.

On the dancer's stage
There was something odd.
The toy man was in a dancing pose
With the one he loved.

Vinathi Prassad
Martinez, GA.

ABCDarian

Yes ma'am and good sir
tis true.
The night is only as sinister
as you picture.

Too often in the day
you get caught up in the sun's violent perspective,
his rays of machismo.
But outside this loose superficiality,
children always seem to turn back to the
starry-eyed magnificence,
the brilliance which bathes mahogany trees
in unadulterated silver as
gentle as a maiden's fair skin.

A feminine majesty
who is but a malcontent at noontime,
but after her solemn martyrdom
is resurrected once again
to her world of nighttime masquerades
where celestial bodies meander
and meteors dance
past the fringes of the Milky Way.

But don't misconceive of her constant
hiding and disappearing,
for the cloak of black she dons
every now and then
is for modesty's sake only.
(she is a lady after all)

But once a month, those *moods* will occur
and she shines for all she's worth,
proving her existence, her strength
because when it comes down to it
the sun is not her lord.

This woman unveils a radiance, heart-rending enough
to strike a perfectly sensible gentleman babbling.
Moon-shine
for the moonstruck.

And at dawn,
all the morning glories converse
in mumbles and murmurs
about her beauty which was so great
the sun, in all his pride,
banished her to the realm of shadows.
However, it seems I must and will
continue to remain mute; in awe.
Because for myself.
I will never cease to be both amazed and terrified
at the elegant, effeminate mystique
of "Luna."

Katie Crow
Augusta, GA.

THE TAKERS

Our minds are held captive in a fantastic prison
A prison with forces so powerful yet invisible,
we've yet to realize we're trapped.

Someone inquires, "Take it or leave it?"
I whisper, "I shall take it."

I fall asleep in the wretched forest of fortuity
and awaken sprawled out in a field
of never-ending green majesty.
Where I can taste the present and superintend
the future ... all in my own ignorance.

Someone inquires, "Take it or leave it?"
I firmly state, "I shall take it."

Coming across an ancient scripture
I find the calling of our destiny.
"The world is a human life-support system, "a machine
designed to produce and sustain human life."
My mind is overridden by the words of fate.
Running through the green majesty,
through the grand rocks, through it all. It is mine.
I was designed to conquer and rule.
I am no jellyfish.

I listen to the water, to the trees, to the wind, to the sky,
to the air, to the sun, to
the particles of dust. I live it. I breathe it.
It is mine. I own it.

I can hear it,
every day, every second,
every moment that I live.
Man will conquer.
Man will conquer.

Someone inquires, "Take it or leave it?"
I jump for joy, "I shall take it!"

I look to the skies for the Gods
and detect their presence.
But staring them down, I am above them.
Mythology claims that I am the exception.
The end product. I stand alone
infinitely apart from the rest of the grasshoppers.

I crave that succulent knowledge that will propel me
forward, like Adam tasting a
fruit from the Tree of the Knowledge of Good and Evil.
And thus, as I taste that fruit, it propels me forward. I
am free falling. Pedaling
away faster than ever – like cyclists completing the last
hundred yards of their
"around the world" race. A thunderbolt.

Pedaling
    Falling
        Pedaling
            Falling

Who's to know I was pedaling air?
Someone inquires, "Take it or leave it?"
I shout at the top of my lungs, "I *will* take it!"

Blind to the ground approaching my feet in a fatal crash.
Disillusionment far away in the future.
Having a grand old time.
Death awaiting.
It is the... the Fall of Man. And as I fall,
Cain teaches me to slaughter Abel.

Someone inquires, "Take it or leave it?"
I cry and scream, the echoes of my voice reverberating
among the cliffs of the canyon,
which I have pushed myself off the edge.

Take it!   Take it!   Take it!   Take it!   Take it!

I fall asleep in a bloody heap of flesh and bones.
But they are not my flesh and bones... for *Mother Nature is crying.*
And awaken in a dark room,
full of thousands of pairs
of gleaming bright eyes.
Staring. Hoping. Yearning.

Man must stop. Man must teach.
I reach for the ancient scripture and spit on the words,
smudge them with my fists and write anew.

But you can't change these things with laws, you must change the people's minds.

It is the fantastic prison that is holding me captive.
Holding us captive.
Me and the thousands of pairs of eyes.
A prison with forces so powerful yet invisible.
We've yet to realize.
We are trapped.

Daniela Shorser
Pound Ridge, NY

TO MY WIFE: YESTERDAY IN KANDAHAR

Our supplies had run short
Under a sun that burned hot,
As we marched in a valley
It seemed God had forgot.

All thoughts were focused
On completing our mission,
It seemed within reach,
We had made our decision.

Yet how quickly things change
By cruel twists of fate
In a hail storm of bullets
We could not escape.

We bravely fought back,
Yet my friends, they were dead.
The blood spilled on that ground
Stained all the earth red.

I thought of you my love
And our children, so far,
As I died in that valley,
Yesterday, in Kandahar.

I will not see you again,
At least not in life,
Yet my spirit remains yours,
My dearly beloved wife.

Steven Brooks
Martinez, GA

THE DANDELION

They pop up unannounced,
Unwanted,
Dreaded by some.
Tiny green sprigs brighten
the dull brown of the winter lawn.
They are the first to herald the spring scene
And they are the last to whisper
"farewell" in the autumn.

Soon bright yellow blossoms
add color to spring's welcome mat.
"Dent de lion," "Lion's teeth" they are called,
Ready to devour that lush, green lawn.
Pull one out and like hydra, two will replace it.

Quickly the yellow blossoms fade,
Churning out small, cottony puff balls.
Children delight in running with them
Blowing the gossamer wisps in the air
Launching their wishes on the wind.

They rise like miniature hot air balloons
Riding high wherever the wind takes them,
Only to descend like parachutes
Planting their glory over all the earth.

Virtue or menace,
Perennial or eternal,
Wildflower or weed,
Gardener's scourge or salad greens,

to enhance french cuisine.
Blossoms that relinquish Heaven's nectar,
A cordial or wine fit for the gods.
Scorned as the lowliest of God's botanical creations.
Yet lofty enough to be offered as a child's gift
And cherished by a loving mother.
The lofty, lowly dandelion!

Joan M. Lacombe
Aiken, SC

OF MICE AND MEN-AND ELEPHANTS

When they are very young
men, mice and elephants are equally at risk.
Adults may reject them, trample them,
refuse to feed or care for them or
just pretend that they aren't there.
But when they grow up things change.
Mice can scamper, leap, hide, avoid harm;
elephants can be stampeded to their death
by mice. And if you asked an
avenging elephant or a scavenging mouse
"What is man that thou art mindful of him?"
They'd just laugh and swish their tails.

**K.R. (Joe) Massingham
Chisholm, Australia**

FREEDOM

And deep inside of me if I could have searched the recesses of my feeble conscience, I might have found something like: Free at last!
-Elie Wiesel

I remember her pushing me on my swing,
Holding me in her arms, singing "Que Sera"
Her face filled with crinkles and character
her eyes, electric blue with crows feet at the corners.
Every dent, crevice told a story.
To me she was a hero; she still is.
She was a fighter, she got what she wanted
but little by little her strength began to fade.
The wide grin on her face disappeared.

The struggle, the pain
She breathes, in and out.
Each breath sucks the life out of her
What used to be a face full of smiles and humor
Is now emotionless and lethargic
I selfishly pray
For her to stay alive
But for what use?
For her to suffer, to be in agony?
Like a holocaust victim.
Exhausted and frail,
she hopes for only one thing:
Freedom.

Jacklyn Lopez
Miami Shores, FL

SECOND PLACE WINNERS

A SAVAGE YAWP

We are fallen saints, wandering
        —toting manifestos of gore
and frank poetry

We gobble up textbooks
        lobotomizing our stained-glass skulls
                with a curriculum of insanity
until we are intellectually obese
        so hulking with knowledge
that we cannot exercise wisdom
    By mesmerizing pages of scripture
but not living it
            merely stocking up on words
    but giving them no meaning
    we are spiritually obese as well
    We eat angels for breakfast
munching on Seraphim with our Weetabix
            they taste heavenly
but provide no divine supplement

II

Our qualms are small

so close we are to contentment

only still slightly aggravated

by minute dilemmas

(like poverty and nuclear war)

Pulverized by pure logic

lynched up with ethics

we are strapped to unholy thrones:

Politely fry our brains

Grappling with mediocrity

we scour for enlightenment

but find only education

we voyaged for the Promised Land

but shipwrecked in America

We've lost the battle

What is the War?

Derek Berry
Aiken, SC

GENERATION APATHY

Punctuation poses as emotion:
Colon, parenthesis, semi-colon.
But can you really have part of a colon?
Only if you spend all your spare change on fast food.
But now whose got extra change? After all, we're in a recession
and nothing comes fast enough
for this apathetic generation
unless it can be mass produced and manufactured,
like Kentucky Fried Chicken- molded
with George Washington's face.

We, "cannot tell a lie",
we'd rather chop off someone else's wings,
in order for us to fly.

I am seventeen years old.
That's seventeen years of mysterious bruises.
Seventeen years of only partially hearing the world.
Seventeen years of reading about romance but never knowing love.

My sister asks: "What's it like,
to never hear the birds sing?"
"I don't know the difference," I tell her.
I say, "We are all born special."
I am only half deaf.
Like everything else in my life it's one-sided
amidst the give and give.

I am seventeen years old
and even I don't understand my generation.

People who read Genesis and Leviticus
but can't even follow the golden rule.

Who smile to your face but call you a hor-
.....ribble name behind your back.

This is not the world I chose for my future.

I am seventeen yet,
I long to live longer:
to feel age gnaw at my bones,
to inhale more than cigarette smoke with my oxygen
And to feel safe in my own home.

I long to no longer feel the need to shed my skin
To find a perfect fit-
to chase after my dreams
and to cease fearing hypotheticals.

The computer screen flashes.
Colon. Parenthesis. Enter.

See. I'm smiling.

Melissa Bouganım
Sunny Isle Beach, FL

BEYOND SIGHT

All shadows fade
in the light of the afternoon.

You and I,
we see it.

The way
a full field beckons,
waving golden, the way pigeons hum
low rumbles,
sticking their necks to the ground.
The same way the spider hangs,
spindle and thread,
bottom dangling from a cracked windowsill.
Connected only to air, to the hush of breath,
to the pure sway of steel silk,
you and I know this,   this way,
how the toneless echoes crooning
from my throat are for you alone,
for you, these lily petals unfurling,
these gusts of laughter breaking a face into
dimples.

We share in this knowing, this way.

The way the moon will always seek
its reflection in the water and
brighten scattered clouds.

Stephanie Wang
Roslyn, NY

WHAT MORE WAS I TO DO?

I said a prayer and held your hand;
Everything ceased but you.
I called our family and friends;
What more was I to do?
On the outside I looked adult,
Reposed and strong and sane,
While the little girl here inside of me
Screamed and cried in pain.
I listened to all the doctors,
"Just a matter of time."
I held my fears and tears at bay —
Protective pantomime.
I fed you, and I cleaned you
As you once did for me.
It was my turn to take care of you,
My turn to help you see
That although you were scared and tired
You could rest peacefully.
You would be loved and protected
By God, angels and me.
And after all the lingering,
The time had finally come.
Your chest rose just one last time
And silence filled the room.
I held you and I prayed to God
To take you in His arms
And reunite you with family
And keep you safe from harm.
The adult that I seemed to be
Was just a little girl

Curled up to her once-strong Daddy
Who had just left her world.
I held you and then let you go
With a, "Daddy, I love you."
I kissed your cheek and said goodbye.
What more was I to do?

**Jamie Turner
Aiken, S.C.**

"THE TINY FLOWER"

Swaying in the gentle breeze,
feeling the whizzing noise of the meadow
I longed to hasten my blooming moment,
but then remembered "patience is a virtue."
There is an order for everything; I need to wait for that
time predestined by the mighty power.
Then it happened . . . .
Slowly slithering through the spread out green sepals.
I looked at the light.
"Thank you Sun"
for the energy you gave us to sprout and bloom.
Looking at myself for the first time,
I saw the eye-catching color of my body.
No painter can match.
Feeling my body, the softness so sensual I blushed.
"Oh My God!
"I am pretty". "I am beautiful"
Then I turned in the gentle breeze.
Looked around in the meadow . . . .
"Oh My"! I exclaimed
What a sight! Rainbow of colors:
purple, yellow, green, violet, red.
Flowers they are.
Like myself but so much more beautiful and colorful,
so many more different sizes and shapes.
Carpeting the world around me belittling my Ego. . . . . .
I sensed a swift movement in my body, looked up saw a
creature fluttering the wings so fast and
hovering over; smiling at me . . . . Gently caressed my
inner self . . . .I felt my quivering body succumbing to the

bee's desire ...... Gently the pollen of love was trans-
ferred ....the bee departed.
I felt my spirits lift, for being desirable
to someone else.
I felt that with my God given talents;
fragrance and color.
I could be useful,
in a small way to this place,
where I was born.
Once again the gentle breeze made me dance and I
looked around and learned to synchronize
To be in tune with my fellow beings ------ all different
in shapes & colors but swaying in the same
direction to make the <u>Music Of Happiness</u>.

Daniel George
Grovetown, GA.

MAY'S CAFÉ

The old-timer at May's Café
Held down the corner booth
He'd ascertain your obstacles
Then briefly say the sooth.

Newcomers approached one day
And sought his sagely views
The fellow said, "What's this town like?"
The old man asked, amused.

"What's it like where you came from?"
The couple shared a frown
Said he, "Misguided malcontents
Who'd snub you when you're down."

Said she, "Hardheaded hypocrites,
Who never took the blame"
The old man answered sadly,
"This town is just the same."

Another pair from out of town
Stopped to dine at May's
Drifted toward the corner booth
Caught the old man's gaze.

"We just moved here," the woman said
"And wondered what it's like"
Her husband interjected,
"We're just from down the pike.

We left a slice of paradise
Said 'so long' to neighbors
Who welcomed us like kinfolk
Showered us with favors."

"The dearest friends!" his wife agreed
And wiped a wistful tear
The old man said, "Don't worry
It's just like that here."

Nick Sweet
Shepard, TX

THIRD PLACE WINNERS

ODE TO SUMMER IN THE SOUTH

Whispering wind through the trees,
they've regained their leaves,
conjure dreams of lightning bug catching,
mason jars with holes in the lid,
shaken to awaken the light within,
sensations unknown to any New Yorker.

Follow me
our bare feet pad silently,
over the log-bridge to dance n' play the day away.

Joyous wonders awaiting us,
in the corn fields where we play.
Off yonder in the fields of rye.
Run fast enough, perhaps you'll fly,
It's glory in the sun.

Sweat dripping down the backs of young and old.
As they work the fields till the sun goes down.
Look above
Watch the birds fly
with grace in their wings.
Cotton stuffed clouds in hand painted skies,
Honey suckle and momma's cooking permuting the air,
Picking fresh blackberries off the vine,
Pricking our fingers
and staining our mouths,
whist walking home.
Shouts of mirth from young'ins playing far off,
adults sipping sweat tea

in rocking chairs on the front porch.
sharing stories and making memories.
Living life simple and free.

Listen to the wind
as the weeping willow
and magnolia call to us,
Come and play in our branches,
when you're through chasing the
sun's last golden rays across the yard.
Come dream beneath our canopies
as the crickets lull you asleep,
underneath the stars tonight.

Today's another day,
Turned fluidly to night.
Life here is simple and slow,
Blessedly pure.

Breathe it in, take it with you
and never let it go;
the summers here
are unlike any other.
Ode to summer in the south.
(Don't forget to release the lighting bugs)

Jamie Boquist
Martinez, GA

GROWN

They ask why I am so grown,
Why
I act like I'm four years
Ahead of my time and why,
Why I never learn the hard way.
"Wow, you must be blessed"
But "blessed" isn't the word,
Life is told to me,
What is to come
and there is nothing or being
that can stop it.

So I verbalize plain lies
And utter "I don't know
Maybe, I'm just mature"
Or
"I think before I do or say."
But I know that's not the answer.

The truth is;
there is someone writing my future
before I get to live it.
Continuously, over and over.
I know what's going to happen,
every freaking day.

It's funny how my very own mother
won't let me live or breathe
the air of non-fiction.
I never wanted

My palm read
So I ask,
why must I be blindfolded?

I want to feel the pain of heartbreak.
The grief of a thief.
I want to fall down deep into the earth's crust.
And live in my own hell.
Then return to my center,
realizing how I screwed up.
I am only a child of course,
so I don't know any better.
But if you continue
writing my life, Mom.
I will never know.

Thank you.
For letting me be the caged bird.
Who can sing but your lyrics;
just don't work for me.

Lauren Welch
Miami, FL

OXFORD BOYS IN THE COURTYARD

Catching the sunlight, smoke tumbles
from between parted lips and with it
the words. You lads hear about old P.?

They say no, most of them, and the
speaker's obscured mouth forms a smirk
—No? Got sent down.

He revels for a moment in their
reactions of regret and surprise
until one of them asks Well, why?

Don't know the details, he says
pointedly, but I do know that Professor
L. won't be returning this term either.

Pregnant silence, then low chuckles
from some and they all say It's
such a shame P. had it all going for him.

Clever Man, charmed everyone he met,
and H. adds particularly the classics professor
and snickers grow into hearty laughter.

From all except S. who has been
rather pensive all this time, and says
At least P. knew how to get what he wanted.
Clever man, very clever.

The laughter subsides and the smoke rises
and the grass rustles beneath their hands and legs
until B. smoothly changes the subject.

Lyndsey Wilcox
Augusta, GA

THIS IS NOT ME

I laugh at their jokes
but still I wonder,
at what point
did I lose my identity?

When did
The hatred and bigotry convert into
everyday jokes, that I laugh at?

Who am I
to sling around the infamous word
that like a boomerang always seems
to come back and hit me?

Please tell me.
At what point
Did I begin to make a distinction
between "me" and "them"?

I feel like a traitor,
glad that I'm on
the opponents' side.
But still, guilt gets the best of me.

My laughs bring tears with it,
that stream
like a river down my face.
These aren't tears of joy.

These are the sad disapprovals
of my aching soul.

How could I let this self-hate
Escalate and bring out something
That isn't me?

Why do I have to show them;
what they want to see?
My friend,
I must reassure you.
This isn't me.

**Christell Roach
Miami, FL**

STRONGER

Use sticks & stones to break my bones,
But did you think you could kill my soul?
You hit me,
Use your words like daggers,
For hours & hours.
You held me down,
Stole my innocence.
Left pain as the only sound,
Shame drowns me now.
My blue eyes are the only resemblance to the girl left on the
floor trembling.
I fought you,
Begged you to stop,
Finally just took what I got.
Silently believing one day I would break free,
Find the courage to stand up for me.
You left me in pile of rubble,
Broken on every level.
My soul was my only strength,
My sanctuary.
That you couldn't destroy in me!
God smiled,
Gently strengthening me.
Knowing a rebirth is what I need!
Watched the death of the old me,
The emptiness I see.
Cried as my soul began to set me free,
Finally able to truly see.
Slowly, patiently I find me,
Love me!

Stronger I grow,
My beauty radiates from within each day anew.
Now I stand before you,
Do you recognize me?
Standing stronger than you'll ever be!

Robın Drake
Caldwell, ID

THE PASSAGE OF A MILLENNIUM

1000-1099
The Genji's Tale was told
Crusades begun by warrior's bold
Fiery flashes lit the night
England won by William's might
A century has passed.

1100-1199
A mighty temple touched the sky
Great universities were nigh
A compass sailed across the sea
Aristotle saved for posterity
A century has passed.

1200-1299
A Mongol lord had now arrived
An explorer bold to China strived
A new way found to watch the time
New eyes devised to read the rhyme
A century has passed.

1300-1399
The Black Death swept across the land
"Travels" penned by Moroccan hand
Aztecs built a city great
A lengthy war, two nations' fate
A century has passed.

1400-1499
A lady warrior fought for France
On distant shores, Columbus danced
A classic book was printed fast
A painter born whose dreams would last
A century has passed.

1500-1599
A thinker's thought that moved the world
At one church door, a reform hurled
The Earth was conquered round and round
Two mighty empires smashed to the ground
A century has passed.

1600-1699
A man discovered why things fall
Another found a world quite small
A fictitious knight into history rode
A man described how red blood flowed
A century has passed.

1700-1799
A stone was found in language three
A land declared "Let us be free!"
Smallpox beat by one man's dream
Industry changed by James Watt's steam
A century has passed.

1800-1899
Great men discovered germs that crawl
While the first phone rang down the hall
Edison worked to fix the light
Drake pumped oil, black as night
A century has passed.

1900-1999
Tomorrow saved by Carson's call
A barren moon felt out foot-fall
A brilliant mind changed time and space
At home, computers found a place
A century has passed.

1000-2000
From ancient iron to stainless steel
Hocus pocus to a miracle pill
From shadows on walls to the movie reel
Arrows that slay to bomb that kill
A millennium has passed.

James Mason
Martinez, GA

OUR UNSUNG

heap the latest high on news trucks
heap the latest high at news stands

unload beets berries shrimp crated north
fill them fresh in bins of shaved-up ice to sell

patch aging walls raise and lower red-white-blue
scrub schools fire boilers shine windows bright

assure the rigs will start to plow the snow aside
wrench blacked plugs and filters haul the wastes away

bring watts and volts to read the sports do crosswords
say morning sir at parklocks health clubs coffeeshops

train chips tame motherboards to script
for heroes at the other end of anxious 911s

heft trays swing doors plunge platters in hot suds
shoulder back picattas and puttanescas

mow infields hawk cokes dogs in bleachers
swish cold brews sweep cups and wraps away

the backs behind gearshifts stairs doors desks
behind each shift the backs   the backbones

John Alexanderson
Doylestown, PA

THE STRAY

Don't' feed stray cats.
We are reminded on the bulletin board.
Which most people read only
after the milk they have poured.
The bulletin warns of cat-scratch disease
and animal infestation.
And one cat outside our home looks like it has disease
beyond imagination.

We have constant warnings that to feed these creatures
only makes it worse
And our retirement complex
will not provide a veterinary nurse.
Yet it's difficult when one of these poor creatures looks
up to you as if to say,
"Feed me just a little, just enough to let me live for one
more day".

I hop in the car for a ride
to meet the gals for a bite.
At the intersection,
we must stop at the light.
A boy approaches,
not speaking much
but certainly not shy.
He offers some object,
he wants us to buy.

His clothes are ill-fitting
and his teeth in bad need of repair; but
there's something in his little stare.
That says,
Feed me just a little,
just enough to make my way.
We search through our purses
so that we can pay.

The object we brought
we certainly did not need.
We feel that we have done,
today's small good deed.

We arrive back at the complex
and each go our separate ways.
I notice that on each bulletin board
It now says:
Don't feed the strays.

Nell Osterman
North Augusta, S.C.

THE BABY

My sister's belly is like a watermelon,
She waddles like a duck,
May the 14th is the big day,
It may be before or after,
He pushes, twists, and turns,
Little sleep

The stork will soon have a new delivery,
Tiny hands and adorable feet,
Petite clothes and toys,
A big blue room and lots of blue stuff,
Bottles, diapers, and pacifiers

Many showers and gifts,
He is soon to come,
Everyone can't wait, especially me
I'm going to be an aunt!

**Taylor Verner
Martınez, GA**

HONORABLE MENTIONS

THE GULL AT ROBERT MOSES

We were sitting on the sand,
packed tighter than a winter's first snow.
When my brother's peanut butter
sandwich on whole wheat;
cut precisely into small triangles.
Became a seagull's prey.

It was the middle of September,
But it felt strangely warm —
even the peanut butter had gone runny.
The seagull was fat and gray.
I don't think it was too concerned
about the peanut butter's viscosity.

The seagull eyed my brother, and then his hands,
busy encrusting the sandwich
with more and more sand.
It angled its beak toward the shiny foil.
Ready to strike.

My brown eye locked with its black seagull eye,
but it never stopped flying towards us.
It was on a mission — I wanted to be on a mission, too.

Phoebe Sullivan
Miami, FL

BLUE

Everyone was tired and surly by the time we made it to
the museum.
We had been
      cutting and running and stepping and skipping
for miles. It was cold. It was
      raining.

My hair had been frizzing for hours, and my coat was
too big.
I shivered and wanted something to wrap around me in
a way
the black & white tweed sleeves did not, but people were
too busy complaining to hold
my hand
      and besides
it was warm even on the abandoned benches of the gal-
lery,
in the white spaces of the photographs.

A group of us made it through the tombs of ancient
Egypt
the colonial furniture exhibit
the Victorian portraits of distinguished noblemen and
women
      wondering,
"were they happy?"
                    I must have stared at this one
picture of a little girl in a
                powder blue dress for lifetimes,
looking at her eyes, trying

     to gauge if she were pleased with
her view from the wall,
     if she saw me the way I saw
myself, posing for hours in front
     of her frame, alone and waiting
for someone else to catch this
     moment, wanting to be preserved
as the wet, frizzy girl
     in an ill-fitting coat for centuries,
wanting to be seen years
     later by critics scrutinizing/won-
dering/asking,

      "was she happy?"
We scaled the steep incline of the building, and half of
our pride collapsed in a heap on the
very top floor
because no guards were watching, and it was the "mod-
ern art" exhibit
and we were too tired and too large and too practical
to look at a scribble and deem it more than finger paint.

In the far right side of the bright white room was a can-
vas the size of the eastward wall of my bedroom
and it was covered corner-to-corner with blue paint.
  Nothing more. Just the color blue.
  It didn't even have a title.
I looked at it for a few minutes, and a man came up
behind me and said,

"It's a wonder they would even put something
like that up in a museum.
I could have done that."
He left me staring at the painting.

I began to think about the artist (his name was Henry,
so I'm guessing he was a man),
and how important
this color must have been for him
to buy so many tubes of same-colored paint
to spend hours and days spreading it across his canvas
to not get bored of its properties, shadows, configura-
tions.

I began to think
that maybe blue was the color of the bowl that his
mother used one morning to make pancakes
maybe blue was the color of his grandma's perfume bot-
tle
maybe blue was the color of her dress, the first time they
met

The color of his eyes, reflected in the mirror
The color of his roommate's sheets, in his forever
un-made bed
The color of his art teacher's jeans, that she wore
three times a week

I kept looking at it and wondered how this artist
whose name was Henry

who grew up in Brooklyn
     knew that blue was the color of my grandfather's
hospital gown, and of the veins that ran up his
     arm
     blue was the color of the walls of my parent's
bedroom, always expanding to me like
     sky
     blue was the color of his car, the one that drove
away so quickly, never looking back, leaving me
     to ask,
               "am I happy?
I kept looking at it, I must have looked for lifetimes,
and realized how grateful I was for this art museum
that they gave Henry the opportunity to share
his color blue with me.
I left that room so light
Knowing for the first time that
blue
was the color of my nail polish
the color of that Victorian girl's dress
the color of the bruise on my arm
     that blue
was the color of your umbrella
that you used to cover
my frizzy head and black & white coat
from the unyielding downpour
of above.

Abby Spasser
Augusta, GA

AGING BACKWARDS

My mother watches her baby sisters
speed through
stop lights and fishtail
onto early death.

Aunt Monica squeezed
a child out of her pubescent uterus,
knitting him in heroin needle blankets.
Leaving trails of cocaine
baby powder on her son's skin.

Aunt Juanita drenched herself in marijuana,
suffocated in showers of vodka and bourbon.
She died 8 years before her own mother.

My family ages backwards,
falls into temptations
of parentless nights
and strange arms
that beckon when we are lonely.

The first time a man wanted my mother,
she let her clothes fall like pulled pins
of grenades.

At 17, she got her own apartment
to be in private as her stomach
inflated with the poison gas
of fetal breaths, seeping from ovaries.

I never understood how my family
sunk into cracked pavement,
but now, I'm falling into the same patterns
of absent parents and empty houses.

At a dance,
my friends swirl in sync;
Their heads resting on men's
breast bones; their lips playing tag
their tongues, hide and seek.
They are caught up by tempo music,
swallowing them whole.

Pelvic bones collide
with the beat of California Girls,
skirts short like blunted breaths.

I want to be them,
falling parallel to bone
of boys I don't know.
So for a down beat,
I can at least make it look like
someone wants to be with me.

After the dance,
I sit in the passenger seat
of my father's car alone.
I feel like my aunts did
when they first began to break
into fragments.

I wonder if I will follow;
baby bottles and crack pipes,
who will write poems about me?

Sherry Reuter
Parkland III

"METHADONE BALLET"

she poaches
in the shallow water
hoping to
steal even a charade
from the
wreckage of lost dreams
drowning in
steel reserve two eleven
yet restrained
as pirate ships sail
hidden hearts
gambling at the graybar
addictions take
love so very heedlessly
throwing stones
on all roads ahead
past newborns
without a single plea
trying to
take her far away
to crossroads
where choices will demand
end results
to tranquilize the muse
as she
dances a methadone ballet

Mack Crawley
Winter Springs, FL

AN EMPTY ROOM

My aunt Anya teaches me forgetfulness
She scolds me for remembering
The kids who beat me up sixty years ago
Long nights of asthma attacks
Stares at her cup of tea as a stranger
Again, I am her favorite nephew
She ignores my sister and brother

Wonders:
When did they move in?
Suddenly hugs my stunned brother
Yells to the policeman
Arrest this man
He stole my jewels!
Where is my tea?
Reads the morning paper
Who is the president?
Am I eligible to vote
In Canada?
Her eyes clear and sorrowful
Your problem is excellent memory
I remember the kibbutz
What the heck is its name?
She cries
Where is my tea?
I want to go home.
They don't make me better.
I am cursed.
This place has only dumb and old people
She yells at my Uncle Sasha

who died twenty years ago
Where are my slippers?
Says to the empty room
Thanks for bringing my granddaughter Emma
You don't have a granddaughter
You are an idiot.

Hanoch Guy
Elkıns PK, PA

HOGGEREL

A cross-eyed cat and a three-legged dog
Sat in a back yard talkin' to a hog.
Said the cross-eyed cat, "I'm a mess, you see
'Cause my eyes're so crossed, I can't climb a tree.
I see some things here and some things there
I know which is which, but I can't tell where."

Now the dog spoke up, said, "What about me!
With one back leg, I can't mark a tree.
I used to run rabbits and an occasional cat,
But with these three legs, I can't even do that!"

The spotted hog listened to all their woe
And thought it was time to let them know
That it ain't all bad for a cross-eyed kitty,
And a three-legged dog can be sittin' kinda pretty.

He asked the cat, "When a dog chases you
And you look for a tree, do you see one or two?"
Cat answered back, "Why Hog, I see three!
So how'm I gonna know which is the real tree?"

He turned to the dog, and said "Dog can you run?"
And Dog answered, "Yes, but it ain't much fun!
I run so slow, or so I'm told,
That try as I may, I can't catch a cold."

Hog answered back in a voice loud and bold,
"If the truth were known and the tale well-told,
That you can run at all is worth pure gold.

For a three-legged dog, it's not how fast —
It's that you run at all that makes you first class.
Now quit your bitchin' and say 'By God,
I'm the fastest dog alive with the name Tripod!'"

Then the spotted Hog said, "Go and have some fun!
Let the cat and the dog have a damned good run!
When you both tire out like a worn-out fiddle
Let the kitty make a jump for the tree in the middle."

When you take a good look at the woe all around,
You better count your blessing anywhere they're found.

Jim Kline
Aiken, S.C.

JUDGES FOR THE 2011 CONTEST

Jessica C. Clark has been with Poetry Matters since its inception in 2000. She has volunteered as a judge of the middle school category. She is currently studying Communications at Arizona State University in Tempe.

Lucinda Clark is the co-founder and contest coordinator for Poetry Matters. She is an award-winning publisher and founder of P.R.A. Publishing. While working to promote poetry, she has been fortunate enough to begin working with authors from all over the globe. More information can be found on www.prapublishing.com.

R. Xavier Clark began working as assistant editor for P.R.A. Publishing in 2006. He has worked on Poetry Matters since its inception. He has judged the high school category and worked on development of the annual awards program. He is currently studying business at University of Georgia, Athens.

Audra Ford M.D. is a family practice physician by day and a budding writer by night. Dr. Ford joined Center for Primary care in 2010. She came on board as a judge for the first time this year in the seniors category.

Takisha Perry is a published poet, talk show host and literary arts promoter. She has published several titles to date including *"When She Motions Hit the Page"*. She has toured all over the southern U.S. promoting her books and can be found on her talk show *"Kisha's Korner"*. Takisha became a judge in 2010 in the adult category. She currently resides in Augusta Georgia.

Lisa Rosier has been a middle school category judge since 2007. She works as a Certified Medical Assistant for Center for Primary Care, she has held this position for 15 years. When she is not judging she enjoys shopping, singing and spending time with family and friends. She currently resides in Evans, Georgia.

Sharon D. Schroeder is a published poet, professor and literary arts advocate. She published her first title *"Salt Water Blues"* in 2010. She teaches English at Augusta Technical College and has served as editor of Greater Augusta-Fort Gordon newsletter. She has been a judge and advocate for Poetry Matters since 2006. Her favorite category is high school. She currently resides in Evans, Georgia.

Deanna Shapiro is a painter and a poet. Her poems have appeared in Poetica, The Aurorean, The Jewish Literary Women's Annual, Burlington Poetry Journal and Penwood Review. Her book, *Conversations at the Nursing Home, A Mother, A Daughter and Alzheimer's* debuted with much acclaim in 2006. Deanna has been a judge in the senior for over two years. She resides in Ferrisburg, Vermont.

NC Weil is a published author, she published her first novel titled, *Karmafornia in 2010.* She has served as Past President of WNBA DC chapter and is currently the editor of the chapter newsletter, Signature. Her stories have appeared in Electric Grace and ArLiJo. This is her first year as a judge for Poetry Matters; her category is middle school. She currently resides in Denver, Colorado.

www.ingramcontent.com/pod-product-compliance
Lightning Source LLC
Chambersburg PA
CBHW031858170626
46807CB00004B/1790